AF228612

CRISIS IN UKRAINE

VLADIMIR PUTIN

Bridget O'Brien

Abdo & Daughters
MIDDLE GRADE NONFICTION
An imprint of Abdo Publishing
abdobooks.com

ABDOBOOKS.COM

Published by Abdo Publishing, a division of ABDO, PO Box 398166, Minneapolis, Minnesota 55439. Copyright © 2023 by Abdo Consulting Group, Inc. International copyrights reserved in all countries. No part of this book may be reproduced in any form without written permission from the publisher. Abdo & Daughters™ is a trademark and logo of Abdo Publishing.

Printed in the United States of America, North Mankato, Minnesota.

052022

092022

Editor: Tyler Gieseke

Series Designer: Laura Graphenteen

Cover Photographs: DIMUSE/Getty Images (left); Shutterstock Images

Interior Photographs: American Photo Archive/Alamy Stock Photo, pp. 7, 10-11; Anadolu Agency/Contributor/Getty Images, pp. 37, 48; ARCHIVIO GBB/Alamy Stock Photo, pp. 11 (right), 14, 16-17, 18; Chip HIRES/Contributor/Getty Images, p. 20; Chris McGrath/Staff/Getty Images, p. 6; DMITRY ASTAKHOV/Stringer/Getty Images, p. 27; John Lamparski/AP Images, p. 59; Kathy deWitt/Alamy Stock Photo, p. 51; Kremlin Pool/Alamy Stock Photo, pp. 4-5, 58, 61; Laski Diffusion/Contributor/Getty Images, p. 9; Mikhail Svetlov/Contributor/Getty Images, p. 13; Pictorial Press Ltd/Alamy Stock Photo, p. 55; REUTERS/Alamy Stock Photo, pp. 54, 56-57; Russian Look Ltd./Alamy Stock Photo, pp. 38, 40-41, 42-43; Shutterstock Images, pp. 1, 8, 15, 21, 22-23, 25, 28-29, 31, 32, 33, 34-35, 36, 39, 45, 46-47, 49, 50-51, 52; Xinhua/Alamy Stock Photo, p. 44; ZUMA Press, Inc./Alamy Stock Photo, p. 26

Design Elements: Shutterstock Images

LIBRARY OF CONGRESS CONTROL NUMBER: 2022934962

PUBLISHER'S CATALOGING-IN-PUBLICATION DATA

Names: O'Brien, Bridget, author.

Title: Vladimir Putin / by Bridget O'Brien

Description: Minneapolis, Minnesota : ABDO Publishing, 2023 | Series: Crisis in Ukraine | Includes online resources and index.

Identifiers: ISBN 9781532199134 (lib. bdg.) | ISBN 9781098273118 (ebook)

Subjects: LCSH: Putin, Vladimir Vladimirovich, 1952- --Biography--Juvenile literature. | Presidents--Biography--Juvenile literature. | Presidents--Russia (Federation)--Biography--Juvenile literature. | Russia (Federation)--Politics and government--Juvenile literature.

Classification: DDC 947.0862--dc23

TABLE OF CONTENTS

Putin said his special military operation in Ukraine was an act of self-defense.

CHAPTER ONE

A SPECIAL MILITARY OPERATION

In the early morning hours of February 24, 2022, a live broadcast from Moscow, Russia, began. President Vladimir Putin sat at a desk flanked by flags in the Kremlin. He wore a dark suit and tie, both as grim and somber as the message he was about to share.

He addressed his nation regarding his intent to demilitarize neighboring country Ukraine through a special military operation. The two nations had a tumultuous history. They used to belong to the same country. But the country broke apart. Putin thought Ukraine should have been a part of Russia instead of its own independent nation.

A few days earlier, Putin had signed a decree recognizing two breakaway regions of Ukraine as independent states. This went against peace

Ukrainian soldiers patrolled their borders in 2022 in anticipation of a Russian invasion.

agreements signed in 2014 and 2015 by the two countries to stop a bitter conflict. Putin worried about the safety of the Russians living in the Ukrainian states. He sent troops to the states to keep the peace following his signing of the decree.

These were not the only troops Putin commanded. In late 2021, he built up Russian forces and military equipment along the Russian-Ukrainian border. Other countries, including the United States (US), spoke of an inevitable invasion.

Putin denied the claims of an attack, but he included another chilling message in his address. Although he didn't call any of the countries by name, he promised military action against those who came to Ukraine's aid.

Ukrainian president Volodymyr Zelenskyy (*center*) gave an impassioned plea to Russia for peace on February 23, 2022.

Putin is known for his quiet, commanding demeanor.

In his early political career as prime minister, Putin was quickly recognized for his ability to get things done. He was a leader his country could rely on and trust.

During his first presidential speech, Putin promised to rebuild a weakened Russia. He spoke of reclaiming glory from former days. Since then, Putin has made a name for himself as an influential world leader who will do anything for his country, no matter how controversial.

He repeated this promise in his address: to protect his people against all odds. Moments after his broadcast ended, explosions were heard across Ukraine.

Putin (*onstage left*) gave his first official presidential speech on May 7, 2000, at the Kremlin.

Putin (*right*) with his parents, the older Vladimir Putin and Maria Shelomova

CHAPTER TWO

GROWING UP

Vladimir Vladimirovich Putin was born on October 7, 1952, in Leningrad. Leningrad was part of the Union of Soviet Socialist Republics (USSR), or the Soviet Union. The Soviet Union based its government on communism. It existed from 1922 to 1991, when it broke into 15 different countries. Leningrad is now known as Saint Petersburg, Russia.

His mother, Maria Shelomova, worked many side jobs, including as a factory worker and janitor. She also delivered bakery orders and washed test

Putin's family and friends called him Vovka and Volodya.

tubes in a laboratory. The Putin family ate cabbage soup, cutlets, and pancakes. On special days, Maria made stuffed buns with cabbage, meat and rice, and curd tarts.

Vladimir's father, also called Vladimir Putin, worked as a toolmaker in a factory, a security guard, and a foreman when he wasn't participating in war. He was born in 1911 and moved to Pominovo, Russia, shortly after World War I broke out. The older Vladimir and Maria met there, and they were married when they were seventeen. They had two sons before Vladimir, but both boys died before he was born.

From 1960 to 1968, Vladimir attended Primary School No. 193. Even though he lived down the street from his school, he showed up late every day for class. His friends and teachers knew him as a troublemaker instead of a focused student. He preferred to play sports and

YOUNG PIONEERS

Young Pioneers is a nickname for the Vladimir Lenin All-Union Pioneer Organization. It was named after the famous Russian leader who helped create the USSR. The group existed from 1922 to 1991 and was for Soviet schoolchildren aged 9–15. It was similar to Boy Scouts, but it focused on helping students be good citizens, learn new skills, and help the communist cause.

Putin has a black belt in judo and has also coauthored a book called *Judo: History, Theory, Practice*.

run around the streets with his friends. His misbehavior kept him from joining the Young Pioneer Organization Program.

However, in sixth grade, something changed in Vladimir. He saw opportunities in life that would pass him by if he didn't change his ways. He began to apply himself and easily got good grades. He was also finally allowed to join the Young Pioneers.

Vladimir started learning martial arts and the Russian sport of sambo when he was eleven. Sambo is a mix of martial art and combat sport. It is similar to wrestling. At first, his mother didn't approve of her son's practice and likened the sport to fighting. After his coach visited his parents and spoke highly of Vladimir's achievements, his family came around. Vladimir eventually switched to practicing judo and excelled at both.

Before Vladimir finished
high school, he knew what
he wanted to do. At first, he
wanted to be a pilot. Being
a sailor also interested him.
But a fascination with spy
stories and secret agent
movies always brought
him back to working in
intelligence.

Vladimir was so
determined to become
an agent that he went to
the local office of the main
security agency for the

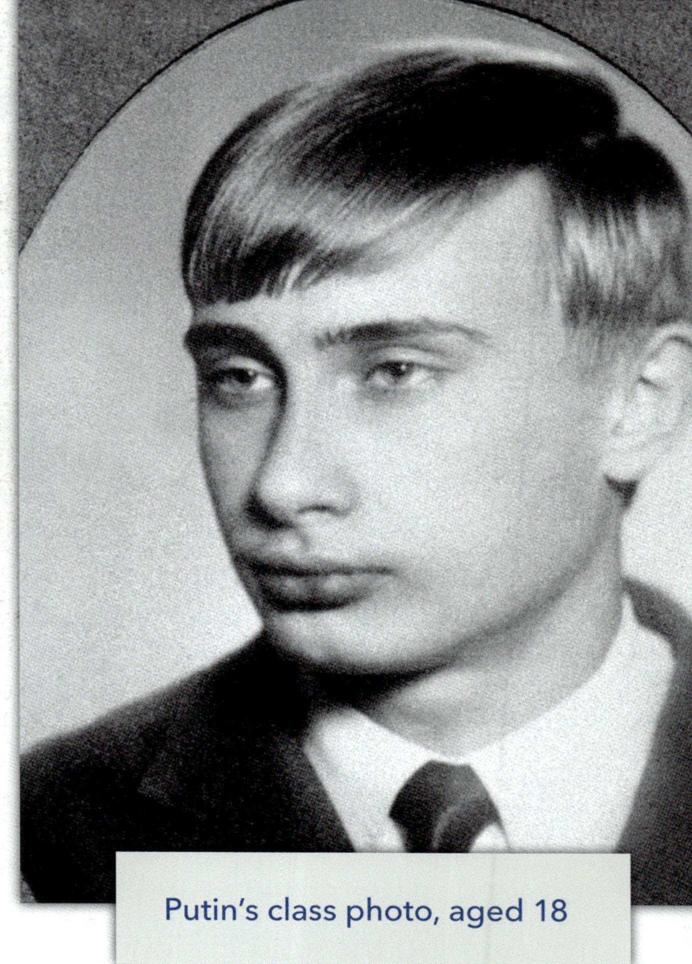

Putin's class photo, aged 18

Soviet Union, called the KGB. In Russian, KGB stands for *Komitet Gosudarstvennoy Bezopasnosti*, which means "Committee for State Security" in English. The KGB protected the country's political leadership, supervised border troops, and closely monitored the general population.

Vladimir stopped the first person he saw in the building and asked how he could become an agent. The officer he met with said he had two options: serve in the military or complete higher education. The officer specified a law degree when the teenager pressed for more details.

The competition to get into university was tough. There were 100 slots available each year. Ninety went to those in the army, while the remaining ten were for high school students. Vladimir's parents and coaches encouraged him to use his athletic skill to enroll in the Academy of Civil Aviation to become a pilot.

But Vladimir's mind was made up. After leaving the local KGB office, he began preparing for law school. In 1970, he graduated from high school and started attending Leningrad State University.

There, he studied international law with his future in mind. One of the professors was Anatoly Sobchak. Some say he was Vladimir's mentor at this time. They would meet again years later, and that meeting would change both of their careers.

Leningrad State University is now known as Saint Petersburg State University.

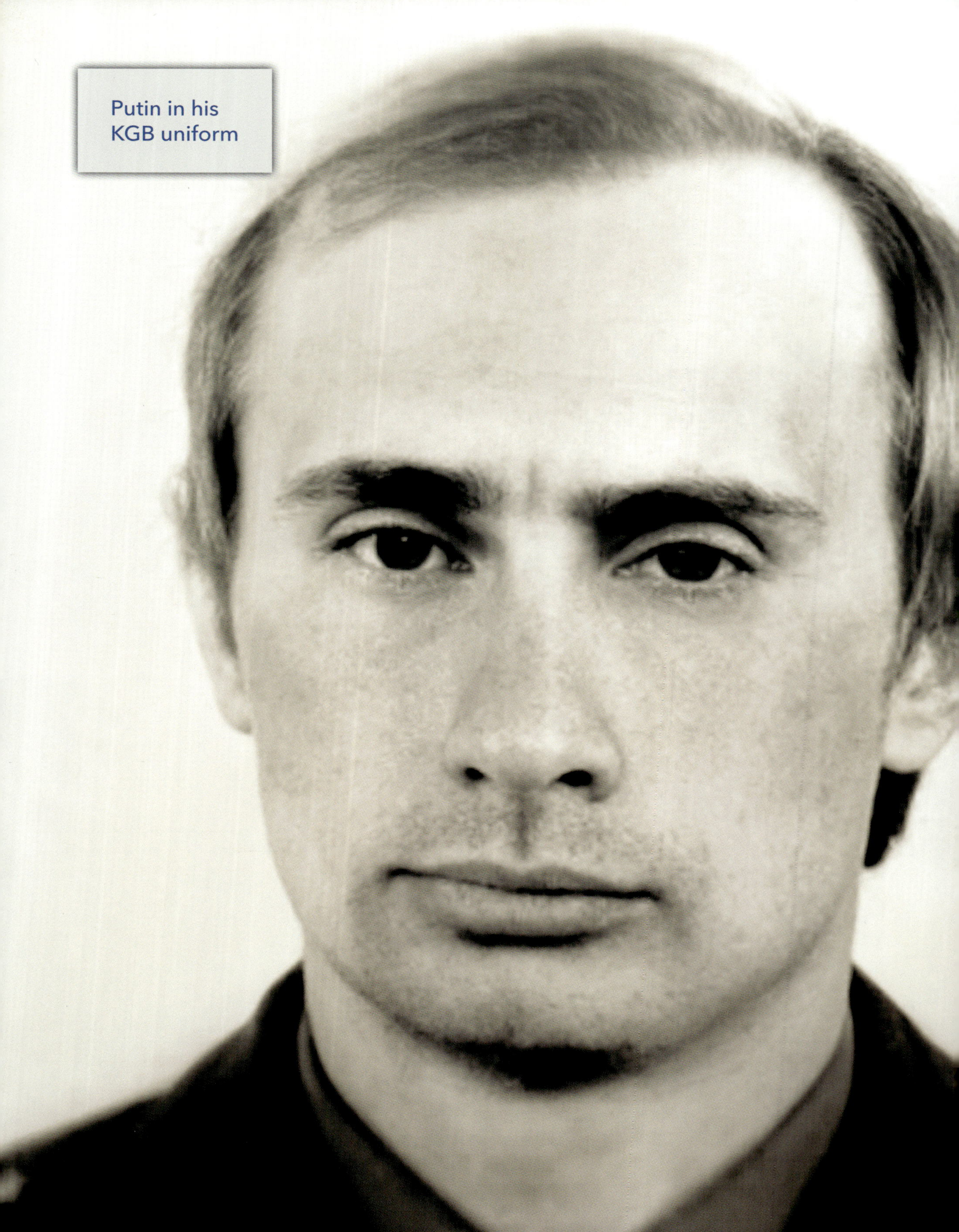

Putin in his
KGB uniform

CHAPTER THREE

KGB AGENT

While Putin focused on his studies, he waited for the KGB officer he met as a teenager to recruit him. But four years had passed. With graduation drawing near, he wondered whether he needed to look for different employment opportunities. In his last year of university, a man who couldn't reveal his name asked to speak with him about a career assignment. Putin knew he was about to be asked to be an agent.

Putin graduated from Leningrad State University in 1975 and began working in the KGB's state security agencies. He moved through the ranks, first appointed to the Directorate Secretariat, and then to the counterintelligence division, where he worked for about five months. Soon he started operations personnel retraining courses.

Putin and Shkrebneva were married for almost 30 years. They divorced in 2013.

During this time, a friend invited Putin to the Arkady Raikin Variety Theater. They went with two women, including a flight attendant named Lyudmila Shkrebneva. Putin and Shkrebneva started dating, and three years after their first meeting, he proposed. They were married on July 28, 1983.

In 1985, Putin and Lyudmila welcomed their first daughter, Maria, before they left for Putin's new assignment in East Germany. Their second daughter, Katerina, was born in Dresden a year later.

When World War II ended in 1945, Germany was split into West Germany and East Germany by the four countries that won. The Soviet Union controlled the part known as East Germany with a harsh government. It built the Berlin Wall to keep people from leaving.

Around the time Putin and his family left for Germany, Mikhail Gorbachev became president of the Soviet Union. He made changes to build a stronger economy and a freer society, so much so that the Soviet republics wanted more freedom. Some felt that Gorbachev swayed from the USSR's communist government.

In 1989, the Soviet Union was struggling to control East Germany. The Berlin Wall fell on November 9. A few weeks later, angry crowds headed for the local KGB headquarters. Putin guarded the employees and secret files inside while he called for backup. But he was told no aid could help him. He had to go outside and face the mob alone. He lied about armed men inside the headquarters, and it was enough to disperse the crowd. The East German government awarded Putin a bronze medal for Faithful Service to the National People's Army. Putin was upset that East Germany fell and knew it was only the beginning of the Soviet Union's collapse.

BERLIN WALL

The German capital of Berlin was divided into East and West Berlin after the war. Both cities were deep in East Germany. They were separated by a concrete wall that ran 28 miles (45 km) and had 302 observation towers to keep people from crossing. Almost 200 people were killed trying to cross. About 5,000 were successful.

In 1990, Putin left Dresden for a new job in Leningrad. He was returning to his roots at Leningrad State University as the assistant to the rector. Soon, he became an advisor to Anatoly Sobchak, who was the chairman of the Leningrad City Council. They worked together on politics and reconstructing Saint Petersburg. Putin helped Sobchak become Saint Petersburg's first mayor.

In August 1991, the Communist Party and the Soviet military attempted to overthrow Gorbachev, but the coup failed. Russian political leader Boris Yeltsin helped Gorbachev retain his presidential status. But it seemed like Yeltsin was the one in power.

Gorbachev's changes had created turmoil in the Soviet Union. The fifteen countries began declaring their independence from the USSR's control. By December 1991, the Soviet Union was no more. An independent Russia emerged with Yeltsin as the new president.

Anatoly Sobchak was known for his confidence and speaking. He died on February 20, 2000.

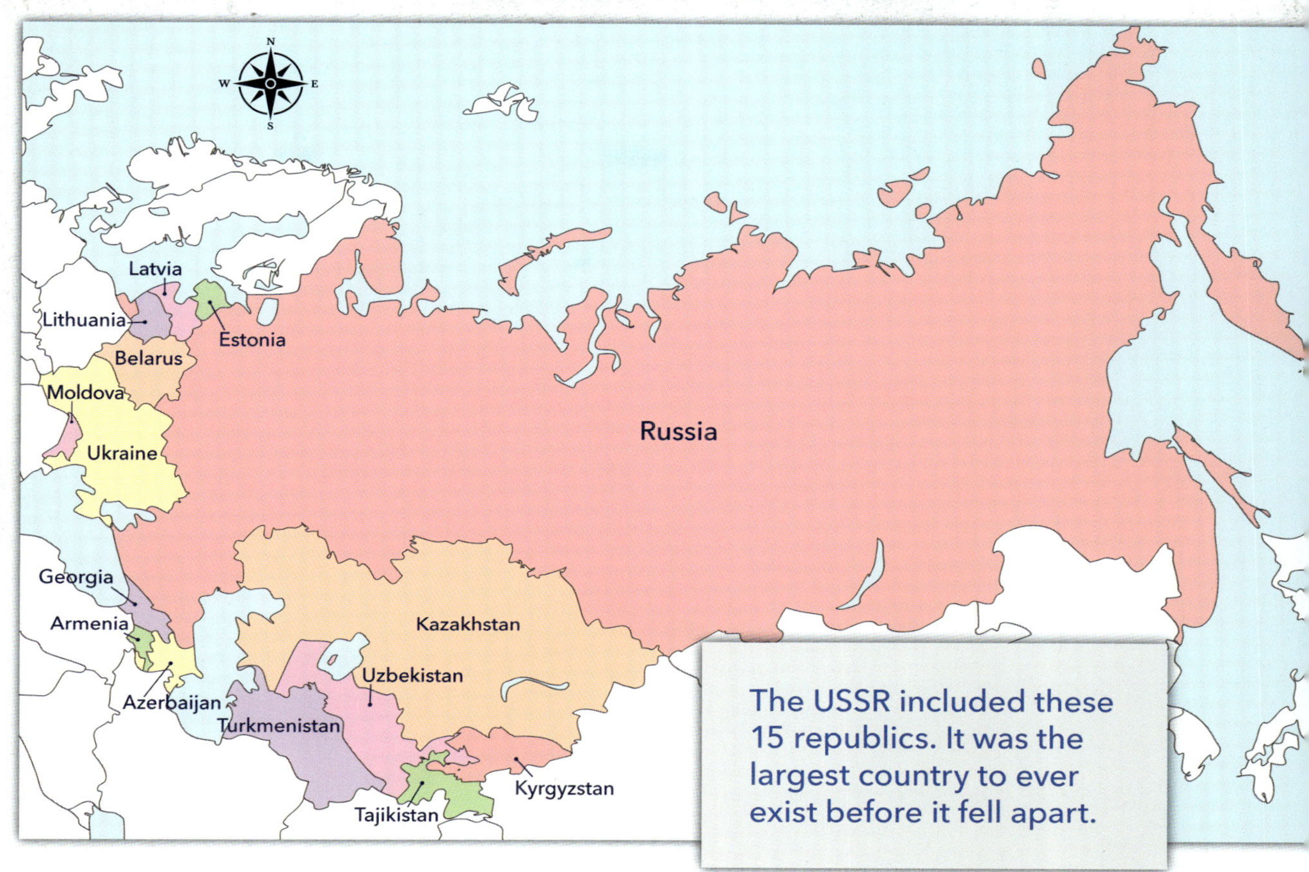

The USSR included these 15 republics. It was the largest country to ever exist before it fell apart.

By this time, Putin had resigned from the KGB. He was elected the first deputy mayor of Saint Petersburg in 1994. Two years later, he started working for President Yeltsin after moving to Moscow, Russia's capital.

Putin continued to rise through the ranks of high offices, eventually becoming the head of the *Federalnaya Sluzhba Bezopasnosti* (FSB), or "Federal Security Service" in English. The FSB replaced the KGB. He also became secretary of the Security Council. It was clear that Yeltsin had a special purpose in mind for Putin and the future of his country.

Yeltsin had fired 5 prime
ministers in 18 months
before he appointed Putin.

CHAPTER FOUR

PRIME MINISTER AND PRESIDENT

President Yeltsin was looking for a successor, and he had his mind set on Putin. In 1999, he appointed Putin as his prime minister. Putin thought this was an honor, but many wondered how long he would last. Yeltsin was known for being erratic. He fired many prime ministers.

Putin thought that if he could save Russia from collapse, he would be proud of himself and his job. He became known for getting things done when he launched a military operation against rebels in Chechnya. Russia faced many conflicts with the nation, especially after it declared independence when the Soviet Union collapsed. Russia tried to regain control of Chechnya many times. Thousands of Russians and Chechens died in the First Chechen War. It was fought from 1994-1996.

Many of the casualties were civilians. A peace treaty was signed in 1996. Putin started the Second Chechen War in August 1999. Islamic and separatist groups carried out terrorist attacks on Russia, but Putin thought the Chechen government ordered them. Chechnya wouldn't rejoin Russia until many years later in 2003.

Putin's approval ratings with the Russian people soared while Yeltsin's dwindled. The Russians were growing tired of their president and blamed him for many issues facing the country, like food shortages. They wanted a firm, decisive leader. Yeltsin was also facing serious health issues.

In late December, Yeltsin called Putin into his office to tell him he was going to resign. This would make Putin acting president until the upcoming election in three months.

At first, Putin wasn't sure that he was ready. The more Putin thought about it, the more he knew it would be his chance to help Russia. He decided to say yes.

Yeltsin announced his resignation on December 31, 1999. Putin became Russia's acting president. The new leader took pleasure in his new responsibilities and made rules for himself: never regret anything and always think of the future. A lot depended on Putin. He promised to rebuild a weakened Russia, end corruption, and create a strong economy. Putin won the 2000 election with 53 percent of the vote. He had been officially elected to the presidency.

The new president made many changes and faced difficult situations during his first term. He divided Russia's 89 regions and

Putin is handed his presidential certificate for his first term in office.

republics into seven federal districts. A representative approved by the president would lead each district. He also made deals with wealthy oligarchs to gain their support, even as he reduced their power.

The economy improved under the new president's rule. Russia seemed to be restoring its place as a world power, similar to when it was part of the Soviet Union.

Medvedev (*left*) won over 70 percent of the vote in the 2008 election.

Putin established rule of Chechnya in May 2000, but rebels continued to attack. In October 2002, armed Chechen rebels seized a Moscow theater and took 850 civilians hostage. The Russian military performed a rescue operation, eventually releasing a poisonous gas that was supposed to stop the Chechens. Nearly 130 hostages died from inhaling the gas. Putin declared the operation over.

The United States and other countries criticized Putin's handling of the situation. But Putin's ratings continued to rise in Russia. He was fulfilling his promises and protecting his country from terrorism.

In March 2004, Putin was easily reelected to a second term with 71 percent of the vote. He continued to prevent acts of terrorism and increased his power by making an announcement. Regional governors would be appointed by the president instead of being elected.

Putin knew he would need to step down as the next election drew near. Russian presidents could only serve two consecutive terms at the time. He chose Dmitry Medvedev as his successor.

Medvedev won the 2008 presidential election in a landslide and took office on May 7, 2008. Within hours, he nominated Putin as his prime minister. Even though Medvedev was president, many believed Putin was still the main power in Russia.

This term was Putin's most challenging one yet. Russia was rocked by a global economic crisis, along with the rest of the world. The country faced rocky relationships with the United States and some European countries. In December 2011, flaws in parliamentary elections sparked protests. The Russian government was accused of helping certain candidates win seats.

Putin faced more opposition than ever, but he prepared his campaign and ran in the presidential race. He was elected to a third term on March 4, 2012, and he nominated Medvedev as his prime minister.

Medvedev was inaugurated on May 7, 2008, at the Kremlin.

There are 193 member states in the United Nations.

CHAPTER FIVE

CRIMEA

Putin's third term brought more difficulties. He spent his first year back in office trying to repress protests against him.

In 2013, Russia's relations with the United States became even more strained. US National Security Agency contractor Edward Snowden revealed many of the program's secrets. He sought refuge in Russia. The United States wanted to extradite him, but Putin allowed him to stay as long as he stopped harming the US.

A few months later, the US wanted to intervene in the Syrian Civil War after chemical attacks occurred outside Syria's capital. The request for action didn't have much support without the United Nations (UN) backing it, but Putin said that Russia wouldn't back the cause.

Russian officials worked on a deal with the United States by assuring that Syria's chemical weapons would be destroyed.

In February 2014, Ukrainian president Viktor Yanukovych was overthrown after months of protests. He fled to Russia. Putin refused to recognize the temporary government in Kyiv as legitimate. He thought it was oppressing Russian citizens living there. He dispatched troops to Ukraine to protect those citizens. They entered the Crimean Peninsula, a Ukrainian republic whose population was mostly Russian. By early March, he had taken control of it. Crimea had been a part of Ukraine since 1954, but Putin felt that it should have been made part of Russia when the Soviet Union fell.

On March 16, Crimean residents voted to leave Ukraine and join Russia. Many thought the Russian government had rigged the vote. Putin held firm to his beliefs that Crimea always belonged to Russia. On March 18, he signed a treaty that transferred control of Crimea from Ukraine to Russia. The annexation was formalized on March 21.

The fighting and unrest continued in Ukraine. Pro-Russian separatists took over government buildings in the Donetsk and Luhansk regions. These two self-proclaimed states are part of the Donbas region in eastern Ukraine. Armed conflict broke out. Putin encouraged the fighting but denied Russian involvement. The US and other Western countries set sanctions aimed at Russia. Russia's economy struggled under the strict trade limits and falling oil prices.

Putin met with Ukraine's new president, Petro Poroshenko, twice. They discussed stopping the fighting in June and September.

Poroshenko called for cease-fires to begin peace talks, but the fighting soon resumed after both talks.

In February 2015, Putin and other world leaders met in Minsk, Belarus, to stop the conflict. Their 12-point plan included a cease-fire and pullback of heavy military. It also gave the separatist regions a special status. The status allowed them to create a police force and help appoint local authorities. The only way Ukraine could regain control over the states was to give them self-rule and let them hold elections.

This plan became known as the Minsk peace agreements.
While this ended the full-scale conflict, the regions continued to
experience tension and skirmishes. By September 2015, the United
Nations estimated that the conflict resulted in 8,000 people killed
and 1.5 million displaced. Ukraine had expressed interest in joining
the North Atlantic Treaty Organization (NATO), but the conflict
ended those talks.

Putin gave an address to the UN General Assembly on September 28. In it, he shared his vision of Russia as a world power. He also said the US and NATO were threats to global security.

Two days later, Russia joined the Syrian Civil War. The country said its airstrikes were targeting rebel forces from the Islamic State in Iraq and the Levant. But it seemed like they were to support the Syrian president and Russian ally, Bashar al-Assad.

The following year, Putin's focus shifted from the Syrian Civil War to tensions between Russia and the West. He believed his country's involvement in Ukraine was justified since NATO was attempting to expand.

Soon, different countries began reporting cyberwarfare and cybercrime attacks with ties to Russia. NATO said Russian fighter jets violated airspace laws in the Baltic.

After a controversial election, Trump was inaugurated on January 20, 2017.

Over two months, more than 6,000 cyber intrusions left hundreds of thousands of people without power in Ukraine. Montenegro was preparing to join NATO when authorities thwarted an assassination plot on the prime minister. US intelligence agencies uncovered evidence that Russia swayed the 2016 US presidential election in favor of Republican candidate Donald Trump.

Meanwhile, strict Western sanctions and low oil prices continued to cripple Russia's economy. Despite these domestic problems, Putin prepared his campaign for the 2018 presidential election.

The France national football team celebrates its win in Moscow against Croatia during the FIFA 2018 World Cup.

CHAPTER SIX

MANY CHANGES

On March 18, 2018, Putin was reelected to a fourth presidential term with over 77 percent of the vote. Even though this was considered a landslide victory, rumors persisted of ballot stuffing in numerous locations. The election was also held on the fourth anniversary of Russia's annexation of Crimea.

Putin's success was overshadowed by the ongoing conflict in Ukraine over Donetsk and Luhansk, allegations of Russia's involvement in the 2016 US presidential election, and other domestic problems that brought about more sanctions. Most of the limits came from the US.

Russia hosted the well-received World Cup soccer championship in June and July 2018. On July 16, Putin held a meeting with President Trump in Helsinki, Finland. He kept the US president waiting for a couple of hours. But they talked for about two hours with only translators present and a bit longer with advisors. Later, Trump said he believed Putin's denial of swaying the 2016 US election.

Putin appeared to have a new advantage in the prolonged Ukrainian crisis following the April 2019 presidential election. Volodymyr Zelenskyy, a comedian turned political candidate, beat President Poroshenko in the polls and was elected president. The two leaders came up with a formula to end the conflict. Zelenskyy was eager to agree, even though the deal favored Russia's interests. The plan ensured that the Donetsk and Luhansk regions would hold

Donetsk and Luhansk are part of the Donbas region in eastern Ukraine.

Zelenskyy and Putin also met with Germany's Chancellor Angela Merkel (*center left*) and France's President Emmanuel Macron (*center right*) in their December 2019 meeting.

elections and gain self-governing status. This caused turmoil in Ukraine. More trouble ensued for Zelenskyy when President Trump asked him to help with an investigation. This led to an impeachment trial for Trump.

The Ukrainian president turned things around by December. In Paris, France, he met with Putin to discuss the conflict. They negotiated a cease-fire and a legal agreement over the Donbas region's special status. They also agreed to continue talking until they could figure out specific terms.

Putin turned his sights to other opportunities for Russia. The year 2020 brought many changes to the country. Putin proposed constitutional amendments that erased the president's two-term limit. Medvedev resigned as prime minister to make way for Putin's new government. He was replaced by Mikhail Mishustin, head of the Federal Tax Service.

The changes were approved and set for a vote in April, but the vote had to be pushed back. In December 2019, a mysterious disease was discovered in Wuhan, China. It was caused by a

Due to COVID-19, Putin had to work on his constitutional amendments over video conferences.

coronavirus called SARS-CoV-2 and was known as COVID-19. The disease quickly spread across the world, and by March 2020, it was declared a pandemic. The Russian government finally met in July and approved Putin's changes.

As 2020 drew to a close, Putin made more laws to benefit himself, such as immunity from prosecution for life. He also made financial and personal affair information secret for all employees of Russia's judicial system, law enforcement, regulatory agencies, and the military. This happened as the 2020 US presidential election approached. Trump lost to Democratic candidate Joe Biden and argued against the results. Putin didn't acknowledge Biden as president-elect for over a month. Their relationship would remain rocky.

Joe Biden announced his 2020 presidential campaign on May 18, 2019.

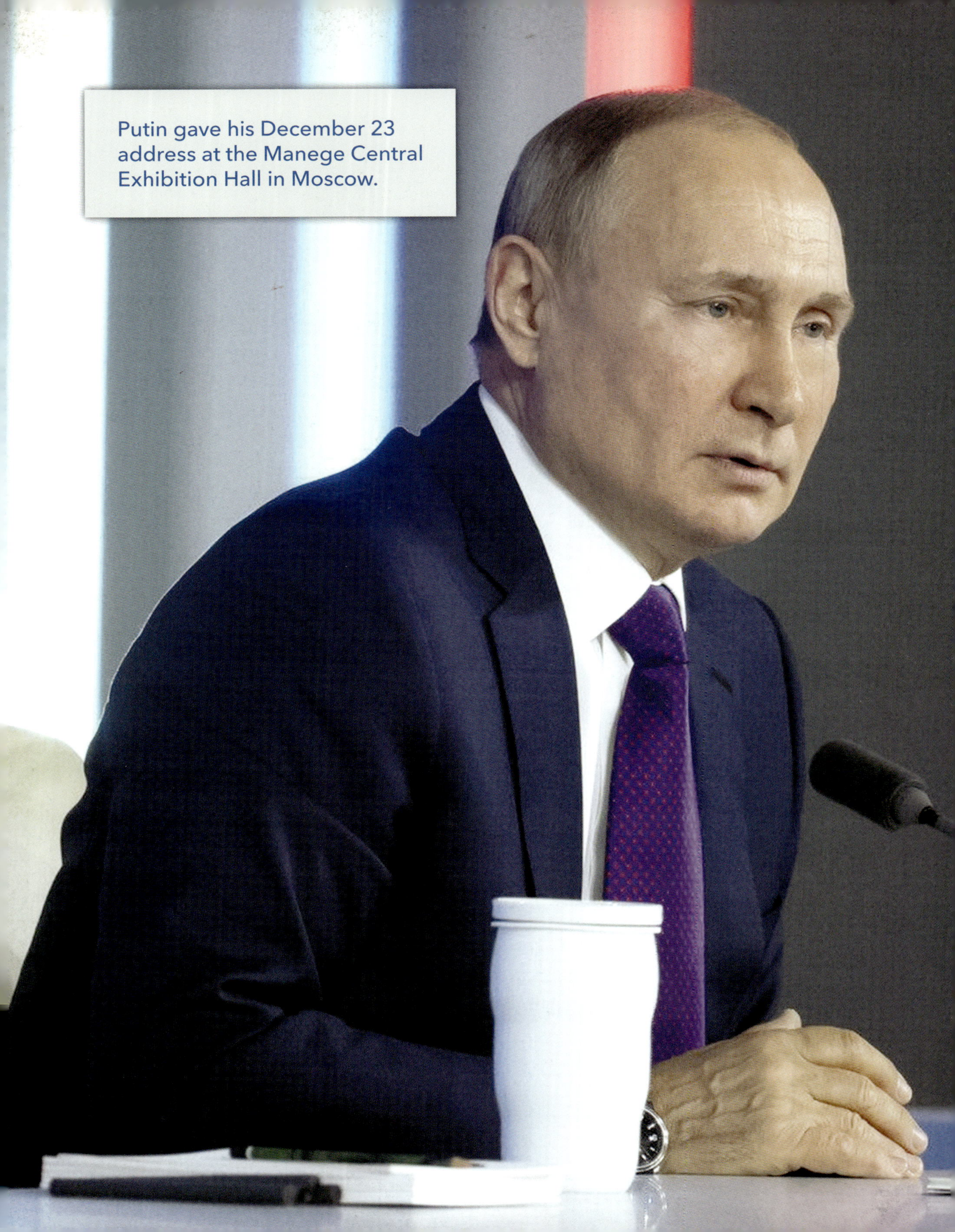

Putin gave his December 23 address at the Manege Central Exhibition Hall in Moscow.

CHAPTER SEVEN

KEEPING THE PEACE

In October 2021, Russian troops and military equipment began building up along the Russian-Ukrainian border. By December, the troops numbered more than 100,000. The West expressed concerns over an invasion, but Putin denied the claims and focused on NATO.

On December 23, Putin shared his demands in an annual press conference. He wanted NATO to stop expanding closer to Russia's borders and engaging in military activity in former Soviet republics. This would prevent Ukraine from joining NATO, which Putin considered a security threat. He also said the West was creating tension. But the West didn't accept Putin's demands.

Putin (*right*) and the heads of Donetsk and Luhansk sign a Friendship Agreement that recognizes the independent regions.

Negotiations to find a resolution did little to relieve the tension. President Biden spoke with Putin and Zelenskyy in separate phone calls, and diplomats from Russia and Ukraine met in January. On February 15, Russia said it was drawing troops back from the border. Zelenskyy and Western officials hesitated to believe the statement. They watched as even more troops assembled.

On February 21, Putin signed a decree that recognized the independence of Donetsk and Luhansk. They had been trying to break away from Ukraine since Russia annexed Crimea. The recognition allowed the separatists in the self-proclaimed states to request military help from Russia. It also went against the Minsk peace agreements, which said the areas were Ukrainian territory.

On February 22, the US issued sanctions to freeze state-owned Russian banks that financed the Kremlin and the Russian military.

Putin issued troops to the separatist regions to keep the peace. The United States attempted to dismantle Russia's finances by imposing sanctions on the areas. But this wasn't enough to deter the Russian president.

In the early morning hours of February 24, Zelenskyy and Putin made separate announcements. The Ukrainian president pleaded for peace. Putin's address announced the beginning of a "special military operation" across Ukraine. Russian airstrikes descended upon Ukraine. The weight of the attacks quickly rippled across the world.

People streamed Putin and Zelenskyy's addresses in all kinds of formats.

BELARUS
RUSSIA
UKRAINE
LUHANSK
DONBAS
DONETSK
MOLDOVA
CRIMEA
The invasion was launched from Belarus, Russia, Crimea, and the Donbas region.
N
W
E
S

CHAPTER EIGHT

THE INVASION BEGINS

Following Putin's address, Russian forces invaded Ukraine from the north, east, and south. Airstrikes and explosions were heard across the country. Russia attacked major cities and areas, including an airport. Ukrainian civilians tried to flee crowded roads, but many were displaced as the forces made their way toward Kyiv, the capital.

Other countries condemned the attack and offered support to Ukraine. They also threatened strict sanctions on Russia, including banning flights and technology exports and working with leading companies on oil and gas. Some of the limits were specifically directed at Putin since it was his decree to invade. The Russian president held firm in his decision. He threatened to use nuclear weapons in response to the West's sanctions. But Western leaders weren't the only ones against the invasion.

Anti-war protests broke out all over the world. Thousands demonstrated in Moscow, Saint Petersburg, and other Russian cities. More than 1,700 arrests were made on the first day of the invasion, most of them in Moscow.

Nearly one-fourth of the 1,700 anti-war protests were made in Saint Petersburg, Putin's hometown.

In early March, Russia blocked websites that promoted war coverage. Several journalists left their jobs. Putin signed a bill to crack down on negative information about the military and the special operation. Protesters and anyone caught spreading what he called fake news could be fined and jailed. This led to both bold and discreet forms of protests as the attack unfolded. One woman held up an anti-war poster in the background of a live news broadcast on Russian state television.

Some Ukrainian civilians were able to flee across the border to safety.

Social media platforms such as Twitter and Reddit circulated posts showing anti-war protests written on Russian money.

As Russian forces advanced through Ukraine, civilians were trapped. Meanwhile, Russian and Ukrainian envoys met several times to negotiate peace talks and set up humanitarian corridors. A humanitarian corridor is a temporary safe zone that allows aid in or refugees out of a crisis region. But Russia refused a cease-fire or to pause the attack for corridors. On March 9, a supposed Russian airstrike destroyed a maternity hospital in Mariupol.

Mariupol received some of the worst attacks of the Russian invasion.

CHAPTER NINE

FIRST PHASE

Russia stepped up the intensity of the bombardment, spreading its efforts to **Kyiv, Kharkiv, Mariupol, and other cities.** The maternity hospital airstrike wasn't the only attack on civilians. Forces targeted health-care facilities, schools, malls, and other buildings. Hundreds of civilians were sheltering in a theater in Mariupol when it was bombed on March 16. Russia said it wasn't aiming for the theater and that Ukraine blew it up.

World leaders were outraged by the civilian casualties.

About 300 people were killed in the Donetsk Regional Drama Theatre bombing.

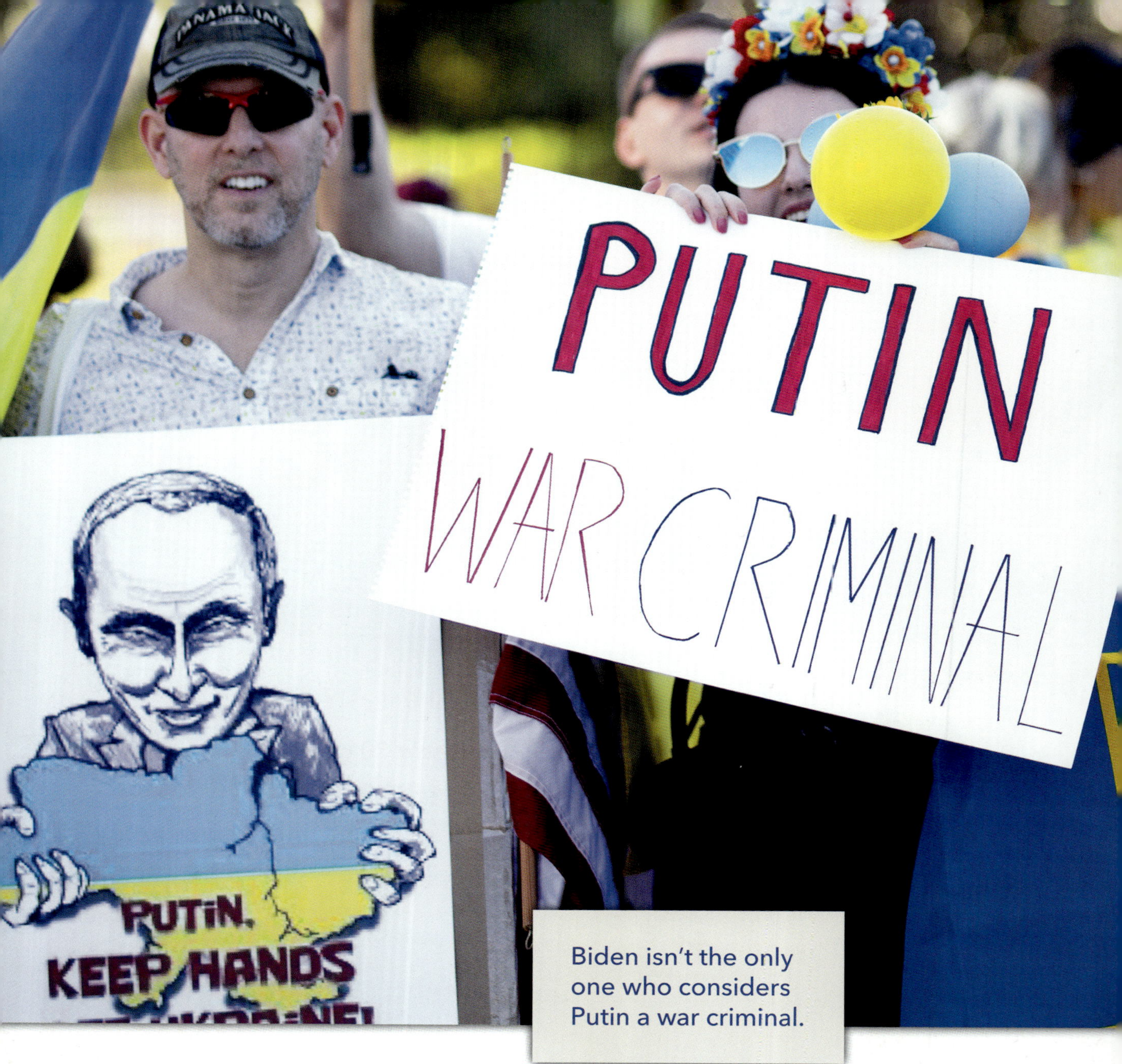

Biden isn't the only one who considers Putin a war criminal.

President Biden called Putin a "war criminal." This is someone who commits a crime during or in connection with war. The Kremlin was equally outraged by the comment. The Kremlin said its original goal of disarming Ukraine's military instead of attacking civilians

remained true. Putin
couldn't be declared a
war criminal by name
alone. A case would have
to be presented to the
International Criminal
Court.

Despite peace talks
and plans for humanitarian
corridors, Russia continued
to lay siege to Mariupol.
Following the bombing
of an art school where
civilians were sheltering,
the Russians made
demands in promise of
safe passage. If Ukrainians
surrendered Mariupol and
other cities, Russian forces
would allow two corridors.
Ukraine refused.

INTERNATIONAL CRIMINAL COURT

The International Criminal Court
(ICC), established in 1998, brings
legal actions and acts as judge
in cases against people accused
of terrible crimes. These crimes
include genocide, war crimes, and
crimes against humanity. The ICC
has held 30 cases. It has over 900
staff members from 100 states. The
ICC hopes every country will join its
cause to help prevent future crimes
and ensure the guilty are punished.

While negotiations and cease-fire talks stalled, President
Zelenskyy insisted on meeting with Putin to stop the invasion. Both
leaders shared their terms to make a meeting happen. Ukraine was
wary of moving forward with this until hostilities lessened.

Sergei Rudskoi is the deputy head of the General Staff of the Russian Armed Forces. He makes important announcements, including updates on Russia's military operation.

The number of civilian casualties and Ukrainian military losses steadily rose as the invasion continued. Russia reported fewer than 500 troop deaths in early March, but it remained tight-lipped on both the number of deaths and its military progress. In the beginning, Russian forces moved swiftly to overtake major Ukrainian cities. They faced a strong opponent. Many of the cities held their own, causing a stalemate.

On March 25, Sergei Rudskoi announced that the first phase of Russia's invasion was complete. The forces would focus on liberating Donetsk and Luhansk and pulling back troops from other areas. Some thought this was Russia's way of splitting Ukraine into two countries, like North and South Korea. Others believed the change in plans was to cover up stalled military progress.

A drone caught Ukrainian forces ambushing Russian tanks and armored vehicles near Kyiv.

On March 18, 2022, Putin held a rally to celebrate the eighth anniversary of the annexation of Crimea. There, he called his Ukraine operation a "heroic" mission.

CHAPTER TEN

A LEGACY

Putin has faced many criticisms as the prime minister and president of the Russian Federation. But the once unknown politician left his mark by becoming one of Russia's most controversial leaders.

When the Berlin Wall fell, Putin cared most about the Soviet Union's crumbling legacy. He wished to see another world power rise in its place. At the time, no such power appeared.

His dedication to this desire would set him on an unexpected path. After all, Putin's determination from a young age had brought him far in life. He had marched into a local KGB office to ask how he could become a secret agent. And he had become President Boris Yeltsin's prime minister and handpicked successor.

Prime Minister Putin was reminded of his wish when he stood in President Yeltsin's office contemplating whether he could handle presiding over a struggling country. Putin saw it as his chance to help Russia and bring about another mighty world power.

When he first took office, he promised to rebuild a weakened Russia and brought it out of a recession. He promised never to regret any of his decisions and looked to the future to create opportunities for his country. Since then, Putin has expanded his presidential power and Russia's role on the global stage.

Putin built a memorial for USSR civilians unjustly killed in World War II. He has said the military operation was to keep this from happening to Russians in Ukraine.

Protests continue across the world in support of Ukraine.

Many Russians saw Putin as a loyal, committed leader who cared for his people. That care stretched across neighboring borders, inciting tensions and unrest in many countries. His special military operation in Ukraine was the largest attack by one state in Europe since World War II.

Putin kept his plans close to his chest and kept an even firmer grasp on media coverage of the invasion. With strict sanctions, growing pressure from other countries to stop the attack, and unrest in his homeland, the Russian president had all eyes on him and his next steps.

TIMELINE OF VLADIMIR PUTIN

Vladimir Putin's quiet determination helped him make a name for himself and his country become a global power.

1952

OCTOBER 7, 1952
Vladimir Putin is born in Leningrad.

1975

1975
Putin graduates from Leningrad State University and is recruited to be a KGB agent.

1983

JULY 28, 1983
Putin and Lyudmila Shkrebneva are married.

1991

1991
The Soviet Union collapses and is broken up into 15 countries. Boris Yeltsin becomes president of an independent Russia.

1989

1989
Putin is working in East Germany when the Berlin Wall falls.

2014

2014
Russian troops enter the Crimean Peninsula and take control of it. On March 18, Putin signs a treaty that transfers control of Crimea from Ukraine to Russia.

2015

FEBRUARY 2015
Putin signs the second Minsk peace agreements. The first was signed in September 2014.

2018

2018
Putin is elected to a fourth presidential term.

2021

2021
Russian troops and equipment build up along the Russian-Ukrainian border. Putin denies claims of an invasion.

2020

2020
Putin proposes an amendment change to erase the president's two-term limit.

Putin has ruled Russia for over two decades.

1999

Yeltsin appoints Putin as his prime minister. On December 31, Yeltsin resigns and makes Putin acting president.

2008

Dmitry Medvedev is elected president and appoints Putin as his prime minister.

1996

Putin starts working for Yeltsin.

2000

Putin is officially elected to the presidency.

2012

Putin is elected to a third presidential term.

FEBRUARY 24, 2022

Putin gives an address. Troops invade Ukraine. Protests and demonstrations break out all over the world.

MARCH 16, 2022

A theater in Mariupol where civilians were sheltering is bombed. Russia says Ukraine did it.

FEBRUARY 21, 2022

Putin signs a decree that recognizes the independence of Donetsk and Luhansk. He sends troops to the states to keep the peace.

MARCH 2022

Russia blocks websites that promote war coverage. Putin signs a bill to crack down on negative information.

MARCH 25, 2022

Russia announces the first phase of the invasion is complete and that it will focus on liberating Donetsk and Luhansk.

GLOSSARY

annex – to take land and add it to a nation.

campaign – to give speeches and state ideas in order to be voted into an elected office.

casualty – a military person lost through death, wounds, or capture.

cease-fire – a temporary stopping of hostile activities.

civilian – a person who is not an active member of the military.

communism – a social and economic system in which everything is owned by the government and given to the people as needed. A person who believes in communism is called a communist.

decree – a decision or an order given by someone in authority.

economy – the way a nation produces and uses goods, services, and natural resources.

evacuate – to leave or be removed from a place, especially for protection.

Kremlin – the location of the offices of the Russian government in Moscow. It once housed the royal Russian rulers and then the Soviet government. The Kremlin is also the name of the Russian government.

mentor – to serve as an adviser or teacher.

pandemic – worldwide spread of a disease that can affect most people.

sanction – an action by several nations against another nation to force it to obey an international law.

World War I – from 1914 to 1918, fought in Europe. Great Britain, France, Russia, the United States, and their allies were on one side. Germany, Austria-Hungary, and their allies were on the other side.

World War II – from 1939 to 1945, fought in Europe, Asia, and Africa. Great Britain, France, the United States, the Soviet Union, and their allies were on one side. Germany, Italy, Japan, and their allies were on the other side.

ONLINE RESOURCES

To learn more about Vladimir Putin, please visit **abdobooklinks.com** or scan this QR code. These links are routinely monitored and updated to provide the most current information available.